EASY MEDITER
COOKI

CW00470240

A complete guide to
Tested Recipes for Living and Eating
Well Every Day

BY

ARYA JOHN

Contents

INTRODUCTION

The Mediterranean diet is one of the healthy eating plans suggested by the Dietary Guidelines for Americans to advance wellbeing and forestall ongoing disease. It is additionally perceived by the World Health Organization as a healthy and economical dietary example and as an intangible cultural resource by the United National Educational, Scientific and Cultural Organization.

The Mediterranean diet is a method of eating based on the traditional cuisine of nations bordering the Mediterranean Sea. While there is no single meaning of the Mediterranean diet, it is commonly high in vegetables, organic products, whole grains, beans, nut and seeds, and olive oil. The primary components of Mediterranean diet include:

Day by day utilization of vegetables, organic products, whole grains and healthy fats

- Week after week intake of fish, poultry, beans and eggs

- Moderate segments of dairy items

- Restricted intake of red meat

Other significant components of the Mediterranean diet are offering meals to loved ones, getting a charge out of a glass of red wine and being actually preparation.

1. Chickpea and Lentil Bean Soup

Total time: 1 hour 15 minutes

Prep time: 15 minutes

Cook time: 1 hour

Yield: 4 servings

Ingredients

2 tbsp. extra virgin olive oil

2 large onions, diced

2 cloves garlic, minced

4 large celery stalks, diced

1 cup dried lentils, rinsed

6 cups water

½ tsp. grated fresh ginger

½ tsp. cinnamon

¾ tsp. turmeric

1 tsp. cumin

sea salt to taste

1 (16-ounce) can chickpeas, rinsed

3 ripe tomatoes, cubed

Juice of ½ lemon

½ cup chopped cilantro or parsley

½ lemon, thinly sliced

Directions

1. In a soup pot, heat extra virgin olive oil; add onions and sauté for about 5

2. minutes or until fragrant and tender.

3. Stir in garlic and celery and sauté for 3 minutes more or until onions are

4. golden.

5. Stir in lentils, 6 cups of water and spices and bring the mixture to a gentle

6. boil over medium high heat; lower heat to medium-low and

simmer for

7. about forty minutes or until the lentils are tender.

8. Stir in chickpeas, tomatoes, and more water and spices, if needed.

9. Simmer for about 15 minutes more.

10. Stir in freshly squeezed lemon juice, cilantro or parsley and ladle the soup

11. into serving bowl.

12. Garnish each serving with 1 or 2 lemon slices and serve immediately.

2. Fish Soup with Rotelle

Total time: 45 minutes

Prep time: 15 minutes

Cook time: 30 minutes

Yield: 4 servings

Ingredients

2 tbsp. extra virgin olive oil, plus more for drizzling

1 tbsp. minced garlic

1 onion, diced

½ can crushed tomatoes

1 cup rotelle pasta

¼ tsp. rosemary

1 dozen mussels in their shells

1 pound monkfish

Directions

1. In a saucepan over medium heat, heat extra virgin olive oil; add garlic and

2. onion and sauté for about 4 minutes or until soft.

3. Stir in tomatoes, water, pasta, and rosemary; season with sea salt and

4. pepper and cook for about 15 minutes.

5. Clean mussels and cut monkfish into small pieces; stir into the soup and

6. simmer for about 10 minutes more, or until all mussel shells open.

7. Discard unopened shells and serve soup drizzled with more extra virgin

8. olive oil, with crusty bread.

3. Bean and Cabbage Soup

Total time: 1 hour

Prep time: 10 minutes

Cook time: 50 minutes

Yield: 6 servings

Ingredients

¼ cup olive oil

½ cup chopped onion

2 celery stalks, chopped

2 carrots, chopped

One 14.5-ounce can diced tomatoes

¼ tsp. dried sage

6 sprigs parsley

1 bay leaf

8 cups water

1 (14.5-ounce) can cannellini beans, drained

½ pound baked ham, diced

6 cups chopped green cabbage

½ pound Yukon potatoes, diced

¼ cup instant polenta

Sea salt

Black pepper

Directions

1. In a large stock pot set over medium heat, heat extra virgin olive oil until

2. hot; stir in onions, celery and carrots and sauté for about 7 minutes or until

3. onions are translucent.

4. Stir in tomatoes, sage, parsley, and bay leaf; lower heat to low and simmer

5. for about 10 minutes.

6. Stir in water and bring to a rolling boil over medium high heat.

7. Stir in beans, ham, cabbage, and potatoes and reduce heat to medium-low.

8. Cook for about twenty minutes or until potatoes are tender.

9. Stir in polenta; simmer for about 5 minutes and season with sea salt and

10. pepper.

11. Ladle the soup into bowls and serve immediately.

4. Minestrone Soup

Total time: 8 hours 15 minutes

Prep time: 15 minutes

Cook time: 8 hours

Yield: 8 servings

Ingredients

1 onion, diced

1 (28-ounce) can diced tomatoes

2 (14.5-ounce) cans navy beans, rinsed

3 celery stalks, sliced

3 carrots, washed, sliced

4 Italian chicken sausage links, sliced

4 cups chicken stock

3 zucchinis, sliced

1 cup orzo

Sea salt

½ cup grated Parmesan

1/2 tsp. dried sage

2 bay leaves

2 sprigs thyme

Sea salt

Directions

1. In a 5-quart slow cooker over low heat, stir together onions, tomatoes,

2. beans, celery, carrots, sausage, stock, sage, thyme, and bay leaves; cook for

3. about 8 hours.

4. Stir in zucchini and orzo during the last 30 minutes or cooking.

5. Season with sea salt and divide the soup among 8 bowls, discard bay leaves

6. and top each serving with a tablespoon of grated Parmesan cheese.

7. Enjoy!

5. Spicy Lentil and Spinach Soup

Total time: 35 minutes

Prep time: 5 minutes

Cook time: 30 minutes

Yield: 4 to 6 servings

Ingredients

2 tbsp. extra virgin olive oil

1 large yellow onion, finely chopped

1 large garlic clove, chopped

2 tsp. dried mint flakes

1½ tsp. crushed red peppers

1½ tsp. sumac

1½ tsp. cumin

1½ tsp. coriander

Sea salt

Black pepper

Pinch of sugar

1 tbsp. flour

3 cups water, more if needed

6 cups low-sodium vegetable broth

1½ cups small brown lentils, rinsed

10-12 oz. frozen cut leaf spinach (no need to thaw)

2 cups chopped parsley

2 tbsp. lime juice

Directions

1. Heat 2 tablespoons of extra virgin olive oil in a large ceramic pot over

2. medium heat.

3. Stir in chopped onions and sauté for about 4 minutes or until golden brown.

4. Add garlic, dried mint, all spices, sugar and flour and cook for about 2

5. minutes, stirring frequently.

6. Stir in water and broth and bring to a rolling mixture over medium high

7. heat; stir in lentils and spinach and cook for about 5 minutes.

8. Lower heat to medium low and cook, covered, for about 20 minutes or until

9. lentils are tender.

10. Stir in chopped parsley and lime juice and remove the pot from heat; set

11. stand for at least 5 minutes for flavors to meld and serve hot with favorite

12. rustic Italian bread or pita bread.

6. Three-Bean Soup with Tomato Pesto

Total time: 50 minutes

Prep time: 20 minutes

Cook time: 30 minutes

Yield: 6 servings

Ingredients

Tomato Pesto Sauce

4-6 garlic cloves

1 cup diced tomatoes

15 large basil leaves

½ cup extra virgin olive oil

½ cup grated Parmesan cheese

Sea salt

Black pepper

Soup ingredients

2 tbsp. extra virgin olive oil, plus more for drizzling

1 russet potato, peeled and diced

1½ cups diced tomatoes

8-oz French green beans, chopped

1 tsp. hot paprika

1 tbsp. coriander

Sea salt

Black pepper

1 tbsp. white vinegar

6 cups vegetable broth

2 cups cooked red kidney beans

2 cups cooked white kidney beans

⅓ cup toasted pine nuts

Basil leaves

Grated Parmesan

Directions

1. Make tomato pesto sauce:

2. Pulse together garlic and tomatoes in a food processor until well combined.

3. Add basil and continue pulsing.

4. Gradually add extra virgin olive oil and pulse until smooth.

5. Transfer the pesto to a bowl and stir in grated Parmesan cheese; season to

6. taste with salt and pepper and set aside.

7. In a heavy pot or Dutch oven, heat 2 tablespoons extra virgin olive oil over

8. medium high heat until hot but not smoky.

9. Add diced potato and lower heat to medium.

10. Cook, stirring occasionally, for about 4 minutes.

11. Stir in tomatoes, green beans, spices and vinegar and stir to combine well;

12. cook, covered, for about 4 minutes more.

13. Remove the lid and raise heat to medium high; stir in vegetable broth and

14. cook for about 5 minutes.

15. Lower heat again to medium and cover the pot.

16. Cook for about 10 minutes, and then stir in red and white kidney beans.

17. Continue cooking for about 5 minutes or until the beans are heated through.

18. Add tomato pesto and remove the pot from heat.

19. Ladle the soup into bowls and drizzle each serving with extra virgin olive

20. oil, toasted pine nuts, fresh basil leaves and grated Parmesan cheese.

21. Serve with favorite Italian bread.

7. Lemony Soup

Total time: 28 minutes

Prep time: 5 minutes

Cook time: 23 minutes

Yield: 8 servings

Ingredients

8 cups low-sodium vegetable or chicken stock

2 tbsp. extra virgin olive oil

¼ cup flour

2 tbsp. butter

1 cup orzo

4 eggs

¾ cup freshly squeezed lemon juice

Sea salt to taste

¼ tsp. ground white pepper

8 lemon slices

Directions

1. In a soup pot, bring stock to a gentle boil over medium heat; reduce heat to

2. a simmer.

3. In a small bowl, mix together extra virgin olive oil, flour and butter.

4. Whisk 2 cups of hot stock into the flour mixture until well blended.

5. Gradually beat the flour mixture into the pot with stock and simmer for

6. about 10 minutes.

7. Stir in orzo and continue cooking for about 5 minutes.

8. In the meantime, beat the eggs and lemon juice in a small bowl until well

9. blended and foamy.

10. Slowly whisk a cup of hot soup mixture into the egg mixture until well

11. combined.

12. Add the egg mixture to the pot with the soup and stir to mix well.

13. Simmer for about 10 minutes or until the soup is thick.

14. Season with sea salt and pepper and ladle the soup into serving bowl.

15. Serve right away garnished with lemon slices.

8. Mediterranean Beef Stew with Red Wine

Total time: 28 minutes

Prep time: 5 minutes

Cook time: 23 minutes

Yield: 8 servings

Ingredients

1 tbsp. extra virgin olive oil

1 onion, chopped

½ cup flour

½ tsp. sea salt

1 tsp. freshly ground black pepper

2 pounds beef shoulder chunks, cut into small pieces

2 cloves garlic

2 cups crimini mushrooms, halved

2 medium carrots, sliced

2 celery stalks, chopped

1 cup chopped parsley

1 14-ounce can diced tomatoes

1 tsp. dried oregano

1 tsp. granulated sugar

2 cups low-sodium beef stock

2 sprigs thyme

1 bay leaf

2 cups red wine

Directions

1. Heat extra virgin olive oil in a Dutch oven over medium high heat until hot

2. but not smoky.

3. Stir in onions and sauté for about 5 minutes or until lightly browned.

4. Transfer the sautéed onions to a plate and set aside.

5. In the meantime, combine flour, sea salt and black pepper in a large bowl;

6. dredge meat in the flour mixture.

7. Shake off excess flour and add the meat to the pan; cook for about 5

8. minutes per side or until browned on the two sides.

9. Return onions to the pan along with garlic, mushrooms, carrots, celery,

10. oregano, thyme, and bay leaf.

11. Stir in stock, tomatoes, wine, and sugar until well blended.

12. Bring the mixture to a gentle boil and reduce heat to low.

13. Cook for about three hours or until meat is tender.

14. Stir in chopped parsley before serving.

15. Serve over mashed potatoes, polenta, or orzo for a great meal.

9. Chicken Stew with Plum Tomatoes and Chickpeas

Total time: 1 hour 27 minutes

Prep time: 12 minutes

Cook time: 1 hour 15 minutes

Yield: 6 servings

Ingredients

2 tbsp. extra virgin olive oil

4 skinless chicken thighs

1 14-ounce can chickpeas, drained

1 celery stalk, chopped

1 tsp. turmeric

¼ tsp. ginger

½ tsp. cinnamon

¼ tsp. sea salt

1 tsp. freshly ground black pepper

1 28-ounce can plum tomatoes

½ cup long-grain rice

¼ cup red lentils

6 cups low-sodium chicken stock

¼ cup freshly squeezed lemon juice

1 onion, chopped

½ cup chopped cilantro

Directions

1. Heat extra virgin olive oil in a stockpot over medium high heat.

2. Add chicken and cook for about 3 minutes per side or until lightly browned.

3. Stir in onion, chickpeas, celery and spices and cook for about 3 minutes or

4. until spices are heated through.

5. Stir tomatoes, rice, lentils, and stock and bring the mixture to a gentle boil.

6. Lower heat to low and simmer, covered, for about 15 minutes

or until or

7. until lentils are tender and stir in lemon juice.

8. Divide the stew among six bowls and garnish each serving with 2

9. tablespoons of chopped cilantro to serve.

10. Italian Potato and Leek Soup

Total time: 51 minutes

Prep time: 8 minutes

Cook time: 43 minutes

Yield: 6 servings

Ingredients

2 tbsp. extra virgin olive oil

1 tbsp. butter

1 medium sweet onion, chopped

1 ½ pounds leeks (about 3 large stalks), rinsed and thinly sliced

1 cup dry white wine

3 pounds potatoes, peeled and diced

6 cups low-sodium chicken stock

½ cup whipping cream

Sea salt to taste

White pepper to taste

Directions

1. Heat extra virgin olive oil and butter in a large stockpot over medium high

2. heat until butter is melted and foamy.

3. Stir in onions and leeks and sauté for about 10 minutes or until tender and

4. lightly browned. Stir in wine and cook for about 5 minutes.

5. Stir in potatoes and stock and simmer for about 25 minutes or until potatoes

6. are cooked through.

7. Transfer the mixture to a blender and process until smooth and creamy.

8. Return the soup to the pot and add the cream; simmer for about 3 minutes

9. and season with sea salt and pepper.

10. Serve immediately.

11.Healthy Chicken Soup

Total time: 1 hour 5 minutes

Prep time: 25 minutes

Cook time: 40 minutes

Yield: 8 servings

Ingredients

1 ½ pounds skinless, boneless chicken breasts, diced

1 tsp. black pepper

1 tbsp. Greek seasoning

1 tbsp. extra virgin olive oil

1 garlic clove, minced

4 green onions, thinly sliced

¼ cup white wine

7 cups low-sodium chicken broth

1 tbsp. capers, drained

¼ cup Greek olives, pitted, sliced

¼ cup chopped sun-dried tomatoes

1 ½ cups orzo pasta

1-1/2 tsp. minced fresh oregano

1-1/2 tsp. minced fresh basil

1 ½ tsp. minced fresh parsley

2 tbsp. fresh lemon juice

Directions

1. Generously season chicken with pepper and Greek seasoning.

2. In a Dutch oven, heat extra virgin olive oil over medium high heat until hot

3. but not smoky.

4. Add chicken and sauté for about 10 minutes or until no longer pink; transfer

5. to a plate and set aside.

6. Add garlic and green onion to the pot and sauté for about 1 minute or until

7. fragrant; stir in wine to loosen the browned bits; stir in chicken, broth,

8. capers, olives, tomatoes, oregano and basil and bring the mixture to a boil.

9. Lower heat and simmer, covered, for about 15 minutes.

10. Raise heat and bring the mixture to a boil; stir in orzo and cook for about 10

11. minutes more or until pasta is tender.

12. Stir in parsley and lemon juice and serve immediately.

12.Tuscan Veggie Soup

Total time: 35 minutes

Prep time: 20 minutes

Cook time: 15 minutes

Yield: 6 servings

Ingredients

1 (15-ounce) can cannellini beans, rinsed and divided

1 tbsp. extra virgin olive oil

1 cup diced onion

1 clove garlic, minced

½ cup diced celery

½ cup diced carrot

1 ½ cups diced zucchini

2 tsp. chopped sage leaves

1 tbsp. chopped thyme leaves

½ tsp. sea salt

¼ tsp. black pepper

1 (14.5-ounce) can diced tomatoes

32 ounces low-sodium chicken broth

2 cups chopped baby spinach

⅓ cup grated Parmesan

Directions

1. Mash half of beans in a small bowl and set aside.

2. In a large soup pot, heat extra virgin olive oil over medium high heat; add

3. onion, garlic, celery, carrots, zucchini, sage, thyme, sea salt and pepper.

4. Cook, stirring occasionally, for about 5 minutes or until the vegetables are

5. tender.

6. Stir in tomatoes and broth and bring to a boil.

7. Stir in the mashed, whole beans, and spinach, and cook for

about 3 minutes

8. more or until spinach is wilted.

9. Scoop the soup in the bowls, top with Parmesan cheese, and serve

10. immediately.

13. Roasted Veggie Soup

Total time: 1 hour 5 minutes

Prep time: 25 minutes

Cook time: 40 minutes

Yield: 4 servings

Ingredients

5 garlic cloves

1 tbsp. extra virgin olive oil

2 green and yellow bell peppers, diced

350 g potatoes, diced

½ tsp. chopped rosemary

1 large red onion, diced

1 yellow zucchini, diced

1 ½ cups carrot juice

370 g Italian tomatoes, diced

1/2 tsp. chopped rosemary

1 tsp. fresh tarragon

Directions

1. Preheat your oven to 450ºF.

2. In a roasting pan, combine garlic and extra virgin olive oil; roast in the

3. preheated oven for about 5 minutes or until oil starts to sizzle.

4. Add peppers, potatoes, and rosemary and toss to coat; continue roasting for

5. about 15 minutes more or until potatoes are tender and golden.

6. Add onion and yellow zucchini and roast for about 15 minutes more or until

7. zucchini is tender.

8. In a saucepan set over medium heat, combine tomatoes, carrot juice, and

9. tarragon; bring to a boil.

10. Add the roasted vegetables to the pan; add a small amount of water to the

11. roasting pan and stir, scraping up browned bits that cling to the pan, and

12. add to the saucepan.

13. Cook for about two minutes or till it heated through.

14. Serve immediately.

14.Moroccan Beef Stew

Total time: 30 minutes

Prep time: 10 minutes

Cook time: 20 minutes

Yield: 6 servings

Ingredients

3 tbsp. extra virgin olive oil, divided

1 ¾ pounds beef tenderloin, diced

Sea salt and pepper, to taste

2 garlic cloves, chopped

1 large carrot, chopped

1 large onion, chopped

1 ½ tsp. ground cinnamon

2 tsp. ground cumin

1 tbsp. paprika

1 15-ounce can garbanzo beans, drained

½ cup golden raisins

½ cup pitted Kalamata olives, diced

2 cups beef broth

½ cup chopped fresh cilantro

1 tsp. lemon zest

Directions

1. In a heavy large saucepan over medium high heat, heat 2 tablespoons extra

2. virgin olive oil.

3. Season beef with sea salt and pepper.

4. Add beef to the pan and cook for about 3 minutes or until browned on all

5. sides.

6. Transfer to a plate and set aside.

7. Add the remaining oil, garlic, carrot and onion to the pan and cook, stirring,

8. for about ten minutes or till the vegetables are tender.

9. Stir in spices for about 1 minutes and add garbanzo beans,

raisins, olives,

10. broth, and cilantro; bring to a gentle boil.

11. Reduce heat and simmer for about 5 minutes or until juices thicken.

12. Add beef along with any accumulated juices.

13. Stir in lemon zest and serve.

15.Tuscan Bean Stew

Total time: 2 hours 30 minutes

Prep time: 30 minutes

Cook time: 2 hours

Yield: 6 servings

Ingredients

3 tbsp. extra virgin olive oil, divided

2 cloves garlic, quartered

1 slice whole-grain bread, cubed

6 cups water

2 cups dried cannellini, rinsed and soaked overnight

1 ½ cups vegetable stock

1 tbsp. chopped fresh rosemary, plus 6 sprigs

¼ tsp. freshly ground black pepper

6 cloves garlic, chopped

3 peeled carrots, chopped

1 yellow onion, chopped

1 tsp. sea salt

1 bay leaf

Directions

1. Make croutons:

2. Heat 2 tablespoons extra virgin olive oil in a large frying pan set over

3. medium heat; add chopped garlic and sauté for about 1 minute or until

4. fragrant.

5. Remove the pan from heat and let stand for at least 10 minutes to infuse

6. garlic into oil.

7. Discard the garlic and return the pan to heat.

8. Add bread cubes to the pan and sauté, stirring regularly, for about 5 minutes

9. or until lightly browned.

10. Transfer the cooked bread to a bowl and set aside.

11. Combine water, white beans, bay leaf and ½ teaspoon of sea salt in a soup

12. pot set over high heat; bring the mixture to a rolling boil.

13. Lower heat to low and simmer, partially covered, for about 75 minutes or

14. until, beans are tender; drain the beans and reserve ½ cup of cooking liquid.

15. Remove and discard bay leaf.

16. Transfer the beans to a large bowl and set aside.

17. In a separate bowl, combine ½ cup of cooked beans and the reserved

18. cooking liquid; mash with a fork until smooth.

19. Add the mashed beans into the remaining cooked beans and stir to mix

20. well.

21. Return the empty pot to heat and add the remaining extra virgin olive oil.

22. Add onion and carrots; sauté for about 7 minutes or until carrots are crisp

23. and tender.

24. Stir in garlic quarters and sauté for about 1 minute or until fragrant.

25. Stir in the bean mixture, stock, chopped rosemary, pepper and the

26. remaining salt; bring to a gentle boil and then lower heat to low.

27. Simmer for about 5 minutes or until stew is heated through.

28. Ladle stew into bowls and sprinkle with croutons; garnish each serving with

29. a rosemary sprig and serve.

16.Cold Cucumber Soup

Total time: 20 minutes + Chilling time

Prep time: 20 minutes

Cook time: 0 minutes

Yields: 4 to 6 servings

Ingredients

Juice of 1 lemon

½ cup chopped fresh parsley

2 medium cucumbers

1 ½ cups low-sodium chicken broth

1 cup fat-free plain yogurt

1 1/2 cups fat-free half and half

Salt and freshly ground black pepper, to taste

Chopped fresh dill

Directions

1. In a blender or food processor, combine together lemon juice, parsley, and

2. cucumbers and puree until smooth.

3. Transfer half of the puree to a plate and set aside.

4. Combine together yogurt, half and half, and broth in a medium-sized bowl.

5. Add half of the yogurt mixture to the pureed mixture in the blender and

6. puree again until well mixed.

7. Sprinkle with salt and pepper and refrigerate in a container.

8. Repeat the procedure with the remaining yogurt mixture and the puree.

9. Stir the soup and garnish with fresh dill to serve.

17.Curried Cauliflower Soup

Total time: 30 minutes

Prep time: 10 minutes

Cook time: 20 minutes

Yields: 4 to 6 servings

Ingredients

⅓ cup raw cashews

¾ cup water

2 tsp. extra virgin olive oil

1 medium onion, diced

1 can (14-ounce) light coconut milk

1 large head cauliflower, chopped in small pieces

¼ tsp. ground cinnamon

1 tsp. evaporated cane sugar

1 tsp. ground turmeric

2 tbsp. curry powder

¼ cup chopped cilantro

Caramelized onions

Salt

Directions

1. Blend the cashews in a blender until finely ground.

2. Add three-quarters of a cup of water to the cashews and continue blending

3. for 2 more minutes.

4. Strain the mixture through a fine mesh strainer into a bowl and set aside.

5. Add olive oil to a large pot set over low heat.

6. Sauté onions in the hot olive oil until golden brown.

7. Add the cashew milk, coconut milk, cauliflower, cinnamon, sugar,

8. turmeric, curry powder and salt.

9. Add enough water to cover mixture and bring to a gentle boil.

10. Lower the heat and simmer for about 10 minutes or until cauliflower is

11. tender.

12. Transfer the mixture to an immersion blender and blend to your desired

13. consistency.

14. Return to the pot and heat.

15. Ladle the hot soup into bowls and serve garnished with cilantro and onions.

18.Chicken and Lemon Soup

Total time: 25 minutes

Prep time: 10 minutes

Cook time: 15 minutes

Yields: 4 servings

Ingredients

2 cans (14 ½ ounce) reduced-sodium chicken broth

1 small sliced carrot

½ cup long-grain white rice

1 finely chopped garlic clove

¼ cup freshly squeezed lemon juice

½ cup red bell pepper, thinly cut into small strips

2 cups chicken breast, cooked and cubed

1 tbsp. cornstarch

1 can (12 fluid ounce) fat-free evaporated milk, divided

2 tbsp. fresh basil, chopped

Directions

1. In a medium-sized saucepan, boil the broth.

2. Add carrot and rice and cook for at least 10 minutes or until rice is tender.

3. Stir in garlic, lemon juice, bell pepper and chicken.

4. In a small bowl, combine together corn starch and 1 tablespoon of

5. evaporated milk; stir the mixture into the soup before gradually stirring in

6. the remaining milk.

7. Bring the mixture to a gentle boil.

8. Remove the soup from heat and garnish with basil to serve.

19.Moroccan Veggie Soup

Total time: 1 hour 5 minutes

Prep time: 20 minutes

Cook time: 45 minutes

Yields: 5 servings

Ingredients

2 tbsp. olive oil

2 crushed garlic cloves

1 large roughly chopped yellow onion

2 tsp. ground cumin

1 tsp. ground coriander

¼ tsp. chili powder

500g peeled and sliced carrots

600g peeled and orange sweet potato

6 cups reduced-sodium chicken stock

300g can chickpeas, drained, rinsed

½ small lemon, juiced

Sea salt and pepper, to taste

Turkish bread croutons, for serving

Directions

1. In a saucepan, heat olive oil over medium high; sauté garlic and onions,

2. stirring for about 3 minutes.

3. Add cumin, coriander and chili powder; stir and let the mixture cook,

4. stirring continuously for about 1 minute.

5. Stir in carrots and sweet potato and cook, stirring for about 5 minutes.

6. Add stock, cover and bring the mixture to a gentle boil.

7. Lower heat to medium low and simmer, stirring frequently for about 20

8. minutes or until the vegetables are tender.

9. Stir in chickpeas, cover and simmer for about 10 minutes or until the

10. chickpeas soften.

11. Working in batches, blend the soup in a blender until it is smooth.

12. Return the soup to the saucepan and reheat over medium low.

13. Stir in 1 tablespoon of lemon juice, and salt and pepper to taste.

14. Heat the soup, stirring constantly for about 30 seconds or until just heated

15. through (do not boil).

16. Divide among bowls, top with the croutons and sprinkle with ground

17. pepper.

18. Enjoy!

20.Italian Bean Soup

Total time: 50 minutes

Prep time: 20 minutes

Cook time: 30 minutes

Yield: 4 servings

Ingredients

1 tbsp. extra virgin oil

1 onion chopped

1 stalk celery, chopped

1 clove garlic, pressed

2 cans white kidney beans, washed and drained

1 can chicken broth

2 cups water

¼ tsp. freshly ground black pepper

1 pinch dried thyme

1 bunch fresh spinach, thinly sliced

1 tbsp. freshly squeezed lemon juice

Parmesan cheese, grated, for topping

Directions

1. Heat oil in a large saucepan and add the onion and celery.

2. Cook for about 8 minutes until tender.

3. Add garlic and cook for another thirty seconds.

4. Slowly stir in the beans, broth, 2 cups of water, pepper and thyme.

5. Bring to a boil; reduce the heat, and seethe for fifteen minutes.

6. Remove 2 cups of the bean mixture from soup and set aside.

7. Blend the remaining soup until smooth and pour the blended soup back to

8. the saucepan and stir in the beans you had set aside.

9. Bring to a slow boil and add the spinach.

10. Cook until wilted then add the lemon juice and remove from heat.

11. Serve on four plates and top with grated Parmesan.

21.Slow Cooker Stew

Total time: 10 hours 30 minutes

Prep time: 30 minutes

Cook time: 10 hours

Yield: 10 servings

Ingredients

2 cups zucchini, cubed

2 cups eggplant, cubed

1 can tomato sauce

1 10oz package frozen okra, thawed

1 butternut squash, peeled, seeded and diced

1 cup onion, chopped

1 clove garlic, chopped

½ cup vegetable broth

1 carrot, thinly sliced

1 tomato, chopped

⅓ cup raisins

¼ tsp. paprika

½ tsp. ground cumin

½ tsp. ground turmeric

¼ tsp. ground cinnamon

¼ tsp. crushed red pepper

Directions

1. Combine everything in a slow cooker, cover and cook for 10 hours or until

2. vegetables are soft.

22.Grilled Tofu with Mediterranean Salad

Total time: 45 minutes

Prep time: 30 minutes

Cook time: 15 minutes

Yield: 4 servings

Ingredients

1 tbsp. extra virgin olive oil

¼ cup lemon juice

2 tsp. dried oregano

3 cloves garlic, minced

½ tsp. sea salt

Freshly ground pepper

14 ounces water-packed extra-firm tofu

Mediterranean Chopped Salad

2 tbsp. extra virgin olive oil

¼ cup coarsely chopped Kalamata olives

¼ cup chopped scallions

1 cup diced seedless cucumber

2 medium tomatoes, diced

¼ cup chopped fresh parsley

1 tbsp. white-wine vinegar

Freshly ground pepper

¼ tsp. sea salt

Directions

1. Preheat your grill.

2. In a small bowl, combine extra virgin olive oil, lemon juice, oregano,

3. garlic, sea salt and black pepper; reserve two tablespoons of the mixture for

4. basting.

5. Drain tofu and rinse; pat dry with paper towels. Cut tofu crosswise into 8

6. ½-inch thick slices and put in a glass dish.

7. Add the lemon juice marinade and turn tofu to coat well.

8. Marinate in the fridge for at least thirty minutes.

9. In the meantime, prepare the salad.

10. In a medium bowl, combine all the salad ingredients; toss gently to mix

11. well.

12. Set aside.

13. Brush the grill rack with oil. Drain the marinated tofu and discard the

14. marinade.

15. Grill tofu over medium heat, for about 4 minutes per side, basting

16. frequently with the remaining lemon juice marinade.

17. Serve grilled tofu warm, topped with the salad.

23.Mediterranean Barley Salad

Total time: 1 hour 45 minutes

Prep time: 15 minutes

Cook time: 30 minutes

Chilling time: 1 hour

Yield: 6 servings

Ingredients

2 ½ cups water

1 cup barley

4 tbsp. extra virgin olive oil, divided

2 cloves garlic

7 sun-dried tomatoes

1 tbsp. balsamic vinegar

½ cup chopped black olives

½ cup finely chopped cilantro

Directions

1. Mix water and barley in a saucepan; bring the mixture to a rolling boil over

2. high heat.

3. Lower heat to medium-low and simmer, covered, for about 30 minutes or

4. until tender, but still a bit firm in the center.

5. Drain and transfer to a large bowl; let the cooked barley cool to room

6. temperature.

7. In a blender, puree 2 tablespoons of extra virgin olive oil, garlic, sun-dried

8. tomatoes, and balsamic vinegar until very smooth; pour over barley and

9. fold in the remaining olive oil, olives, and cilantro.

10. Refrigerate, covered, until chilled.

11. Stir to mix well before serving.

24.Mediterranean Quinoa Salad

Total time: 35 minutes

Prep time: 15 minutes

Cook time: 20 minutes

Yield: 4 servings

Ingredients

1 clove garlic, smashed

2 cups water

2 cubes chicken bouillon

1 cup uncooked quinoa

½ cup chopped Kalamata olives

1 large red onion, diced

2 large chicken breasts (cooked), diced

1 large green bell pepper, diced

½ cup crumbled feta cheese

¼ cup chopped fresh chives

¼ cup chopped fresh parsley

½ tsp. sea salt

¼ cup extra virgin olive oil

1 tbsp. balsamic vinegar

⅔ cup fresh lemon juice

Directions

1. Combine garlic clove, water, and bouillon cubes in a saucepan; bring the

2. mixture to a gentle boil over medium-low heat.

3. Stir in quinoa and simmer, covered, for about 20 minutes or until the water

4. has been absorbed and quinoa is tender.

5. Discard garlic clove and transfer the cooked quinoa to a large bowl.

6. Stir in olives, onion, chicken, bell pepper, feta cheese, chives, parsley, sea

7. salt, extra virgin olive oil, balsamic vinegar, and lemon juice.

8. Serve warm or chilled.

25.Healthy Greek Salad

Total time: 15 minutes

Prep time: 15 minutes

Cook time: 0 minutes

Yield: 6 servings

Ingredients

1 small red onion, chopped

2 cucumbers, peeled and chopped

3 large ripe tomatoes, chopped

4 tsp. freshly squeezed lemon juice

¼ cup extra virgin olive oil

1 ½ tsp. dried oregano

Sea salt

Ground black pepper

6 pitted and sliced black Greek olives

1 cup crumbled feta cheese

Directions

1. Combine onion, cucumber, and tomatoes in a shallow salad bowl; sprinkle

2. with lemon juice, extra virgin olive, oregano, sea salt and black pepper.

3. Sprinkle the olives and feta over the salad and serve immediately.

26.Almond, Mint and Kashi Salad

Total time: 1 hour 35 minutes

Prep time: 15 minutes

Cook time: 1 hour

Cooling time: 20 minutes

Yield: 4 servings

Ingredients

4 tbsp. extra virgin olive oil, divided, add more for drizzling

1 small onion, finely chopped

Sea salt, to taste

Freshly ground black pepper, to taste

2 cups water

1 cup Kashi 7-Whole Grain Pilaf

2 bay leaves

3 tbsp. fresh lemon juice

5 tbsp. sliced natural almonds, divided

8 cherry tomatoes, quartered

¼ cup chopped parsley

¼ cup chopped fresh mint

4 large romaine leaves

Directions

1. Heat 2 tablespoons of extra virgin olive oil in a large saucepan set over

2. medium heat.

3. Add onion, sea salt and pepper and cook, stirring occasionally, for about 5

4. minutes or until lightly browned and tender.

5. Stir in 2 cups of water, Kashi, bay leaves, sea salt and pepper; bring the

6. mixture to a rolling boil, lower heat to a simmer and cook, covered, for

7. about 40 minutes or until Kashi is tender.

8. Transfer to a large bowl and discard bay leaves, and then stir in the

9. remaining extra virgin olive oil, and lemon juice.

10. Let sit for at least 20 minutes or until cooled to room temperature.

11. Adjust the seasoning if desired and add 4 tablespoons almonds, tomatoes,

12. parsley, and mint; toss to mix well.

13. Place one romaine leaf on each of the four plates and spoon the mixture into

14. the center of the leaves; drizzle with extra virgin olive oil and sprinkle with

15. the remaining almonds.

27.Chickpea Salad

Total time: 1 hour, 20 minutes

Prep time: 10 minutes

Cook time: 40 minutes

Standing time: 30 minutes

Yield: 6 servings

Ingredients

1 ½ cups dried chickpeas, soaked and liquid reserved

1 ¼ tsp. sea salt, divided

1 garlic clove, minced

2 tbsp. extra virgin olive oil

3 tbsp. sherry vinegar

16 crushed whole black peppercorns

¾ tsp. dried oregano

3 scallions, sliced into ½-inch pieces

2 carrots (4 ounces), cut into ½-inch dice

1 cup diced green bell pepper

½ English cucumber, peeled and diced

2 cups halved cherry tomatoes

2 tbsp. shredded fresh basil

3 tbsp. chopped fresh parsley

Directions

1. Combine the chickpeas and soaking liquid in a large pot and season with ¾

2. teaspoons of sea salt.

3. Bring the mixture to a moderate boil over medium heat. Lower heat to a

4. simmer and cook, stirring occasionally, for about 40 minutes or until the

5. chickpeas are tender; drain and transfer to a large bowl.

6. In the meantime, mash together garlic and salt to form a paste;

transfer to a

7. separate bowl and stir in extra virgin olive oil, vinegar, peppercorns, and

8. oregano to make the dressing.

9. Pour the garlic dressing over the chickpeas and let stand for at least 30

10. minutes, stirring once.

11. Toss in scallions, carrots, bell pepper, cucumber, tomatoes, basil, and

12. parsley.

13. Serve.

28.Italian Bread Salad

Total time: 2 hours 30 minutes

Prep time: 25 minutes, plus 2 hours Refrigerator time

Cook time: 5 minutes

Yield: 4 servings

Ingredients

3 tbsp. freshly squeezed lemon juice

2 tbsp. extra virgin olive oil

Sea salt

Freshly ground pepper

1 red onion, halved and sliced

1 bulb fennel, stalks removed and sliced

1 peeled English cucumber, sliced

1 ½ pounds diced tomatoes

⅓ cup pitted Kalamata olives, halved

4 slices whole-wheat country bread

1 garlic clove, peeled and halved

4 ounces shaved ricotta salata cheese

½ cup fresh basil leaves

Directions

1. Whisk together lemon juice and extra virgin olive oil in a large bowl;

2. season with sea salt and black pepper.

3. Stir in onion, fennel, cucumber, tomatoes, and olives; toss to combine and

4. refrigerate for about 2 hours.

5. When ready, heat your broiler with the rack positioned 4 inches from heat

6. and toast the bread on a baking sheet for about 2 minutes per side or until

7. lightly browned.

8. Transfer the toasted bread to a work surface and rub with the

cut garlic and

9. cut it into 2-inch pieces.

10. Divide the bread among four shallow bowls and top with the tomato salad;

11. sprinkle with cheese and basil to serve.

29.Bulgur Salad

Total time: 30 minutes

Prep time: 10 minutes

Cook time: 20 minutes

Yield: 4 servings

Ingredients

1 tbsp. unsalted butter

2 tbsp. extra virgin olive oil, divided

2 cups bulgur

4 cups water

¼ tsp. sea salt

1 medium cucumber, deseeded and chopped

¼ cup dill, chopped

1 handful black olives, pitted and chopped

2 tsp. red wine vinegar

Directions

1. Place a saucepan over medium heat and add 1 tbsp. of butter and 1 tbsp. of

2. olive oil.

3. Toast the bulgur in the oil until it turns golden brown and starts to crackle.

4. Add 4 cups of water to the saucepan and season with the salt.

5. Cover the saucepan and simmer until all the water gets absorbed for about

6. 20 minutes.

7. In a mixing bowl, combine the chopped cucumber with dill, olives, red

8. wine vinegar and the remaining olive oil.

9. Serve this over the bulgur.

30.Greek Salad

Total time: 20 minutes

Prep time: 20 minutes

Cook time: 0 minutes

Yield: 4 servings

Ingredients

Juice of 1 lemon

6 tbsp. extra virgin olive oil

Black pepper to taste, ground

1 tsp. oregano, dried

1 head romaine lettuce, washed, dried and chopped

1 red bell pepper, chopped

1 green bell pepper, chopped

1 cucumber, sliced

2 tomatoes, chopped

1 cup feta cheese, crumbled

1 red onion, thinly sliced

1 can black olives, pitted

Directions

1. Whisk together the lemon juice, olive oil, pepper and oregano in a small

2. bowl.

3. In a large bowl, combine the lettuce, bell peppers, cucumber, tomatoes,

4. cheese and onion.

5. Pour the salad dressing into this bowl and toss until evenly coated with the

6. dressing, then serve.

31.Potato Salad

Total time: 24 minutes

Prep time: 10 minutes

Cook time: 14 minutes

Yield: 4 servings

Ingredients

5 medium potatoes, peeled and diced

Coarse salt, to taste

¼ onion

3 tbsp. yellow mustard

2 cups mayonnaise

1 tsp. paprika, sweet

1 tsp. Tabasco

2 scallions, thinly sliced

Directions

1. Pour some water in a saucepan and place over medium heat.

2. Add the potatoes, season with coarse salt and boil for around 10 minutes

3. until tender.

4. Drain the water and return the saucepan to the heat to dry them out.

5. Let the potatoes cool to room temperature.

6. Grate the onion in a mixing bowl, add mustard, mayo, paprika and the hot

7. sauce and mix well.

8. Add the potatoes to the bowl and toss until evenly coated.

9. Divide among four bowls and top with the sliced scallions.

32.Mediterranean Green Salad

Total time: 25 minutes

Prep time: 15 minutes

Cook time: 10 minutes

Yield: 4 servings

Ingredients

½ loaf rustic sourdough bread

¼ tsp. paprika

2 tbsp. manchego, finely grated

7 tbsp. extra virgin olive oil, divided

1 ½ tbsp. sherry vinegar

½ tsp. sea salt

1 tsp. freshly ground black pepper

1 tsp. Dijon mustard

5 cups mixed baby greens

¾ cup green olives, pitted and halved

12 thin slices of Serrano ham, roughly chopped

Directions

1. Cut the bread into bite-sized cubes and set aside.

2. Preheat oven to 400°F.

3. In a mixing bowl, combine paprika, manchego and 6 tbsps. of olive oil.

4. Add the bread cubes and toss them until they are evenly coated with the

5. flavored oil.

6. Arrange the bread on a baking sheet and bake for about 8 minutes until

7. golden brown and let the bread cool.

8. In a separate bowl, combine the vinegar, salt, pepper, mustard and the

9. remaining olive oil.

10. Add this mixture to a larger bowl containing the greens until

they are

11. lightly coated with the vinaigrette.

12. Add all the other ingredients and the croutons and toss well.

13. Serve the salad on four plates.

14. This salad has an amazing taste and leaves you energized to face the

15. remaining part of the day.

33.Chickpea Salad with Yogurt Dressing

Total time: 30 minutes

Prep time: 30 minutes

Cook time: 0 minutes

Yield: 4 servings

Ingredients

Dressing

1 tbsp. freshly squeezed lemon juice

1 cup plain nonfat Greek yogurt

¼ tsp. cayenne pepper

1½ tsp. curry powder

Salad

2 15-oz. cans chickpeas, rinsed and drained

1 cup diced red apple

90

½ cup diced celery

¼ cup chopped walnuts

¼ cup thinly sliced green onions

⅓ cup raisins

½ cup chopped fresh parsley

2 lemon wedges

Directions

1. **Make dressing:** In a small bowl, whisk together lemon juice, yogurt, cayenne,

2. and curry powder until well combined.

3. **Make salad:** In a large bowl, toss together chickpeas, apple, celery, walnuts,

4. green onions, raisins, and parsley.

5. Gently fold in the dressing and season with sea salt and pepper.

6. Serve garnished with lemon wedges.

34. Warm Lentil Salad

Total time: 20 minutes

Prep time: 10 minutes

Cook time: 10 minutes

Yield: 4 servings

Ingredients

3 tbsp. extra virgin olive oil

1 ½ cups thinly sliced leeks

2 tsp. whole-grain mustard

2 tbsp. sherry vinegar

2 cups cooked lentils

1 ½ cups red grapes, halved

¼ cup chopped roasted pistachios

¼ cup crumbled feta

3 tbsp. finely chopped parsley

3 tbsp. finely chopped mint

Directions

1. In a skillet, heat extra virgin olive oil over medium heat; add leeks and

2. sauté, stirring, for about 9 minutes or until translucent and tender.

3. Remove the pan from heat and stir in mustard and sherry vinegar.

4. In a large bowl, combine the leek mixture, lentils, grapes, pistachios, mint,

5. parsley, sea salt, and pepper.

6. Top with feta and enjoy!

35.Chicken Bruschetta

Total time: 30 minutes

Prep time: 10 minutes

Cook time: 20 minutes

Yield: 4 servings

Ingredients

5ml olive oil, divided

1 boneless, skinless chicken breast

80g cherry tomatoes

5ml balsamic vinegar

10g fresh basil leaves

1 small cloves garlic, minced

1 small onions, chopped

Directions

1. Add half of the oil to the skillet and cook chicken over medium heat.

2. In the meantime, cut basil leaves into slivers and prepare the vegetables.

3. Heat the remaining oil and sauté garlic and onion for about 3 minutes.

4. Stir in basil and tomatoes for about 5 minutes.

5. Stir in vinegar.

6. Cook until heated through and serve the chicken topped with onion and

7. tomato mixture.

36.Coconut Chicken

Total time: 30 minutes

Prep time: 20 minutes

Cook time: 10 minutes

Yield: 4 servings

Ingredients

20g coconut, shredded

30g almond flour

1 tsp. sea salt

1 small egg

100g chicken breast, boneless, skinless

7.5 ml coconut oil

Directions

1. In a bowl, combine shredded coconut, almond flour and sea salt.

2. In a separate bowl, beat the egg; dip the chicken in the egg and roll in the

3. flour mixture until well coated.

4. Add coconut oil to a pan set over medium heat and fry the chicken until the

5. crust begins to brown.

6. Transfer the chicken to the oven and bake at 350°F for about 10 minutes.

37.Turkey Burgers

Total time: 25 minutes

Prep time: 15 minutes

Cook time: 10 minutes

Yield: 4 servings

Ingredients

1 large egg white

1 cup red onion, chopped

¾ cup fresh mint, chopped

½ cup dried bread crumbs

1 tsp. dill, dried

⅓ cup feta cheese, crumbled

¾ kg turkey, ground

Cooking spray

4 hamburger buns, split

1 red bell pepper, roasted and cut in strips

2 tbsp. fresh lime juice

Directions

1. Lightly beat the egg white in a bowl and add onion, mint, breadcrumbs, dill,

2. cheese, turkey and lime juice, mix well then divide the turkey mixture into

3. four equal burger patties.

4. Spray a very large nonstick skillet with cooking spray and heat on medium-high position.

5. Carefully place the patties in the skillet and cook for 8 minutes on each side

6. or according to preference.

7. Once cooked, place the burgers on the sliced buns and top with pepper

8. strips.

38. Chicken with Greek Salad

Total time: 25 minutes

Prep time: 25 minutes

Cook time: 0 minutes

Yield: 4 servings

Ingredients

2 tbsp. extra virgin olive oil

⅓ cup red-wine vinegar

1 tsp. garlic powder

1 tbsp. chopped fresh dill

¼ tsp. sea salt

¼ tsp. freshly ground pepper

2 ½ cups chopped cooked chicken

6 cups chopped romaine lettuce

1 cucumber, peeled, seeded and chopped

2 medium tomatoes, chopped

½ cup crumbled feta cheese

½ cup sliced ripe black olives

½ cup finely chopped red onion

Directions

1. In a large bowl, whisk together extra virgin olive oil, vinegar, garlic

2. powder, dill, sea salt and pepper.

3. Add chicken, lettuce, cucumber, tomatoes, feta, and olives and toss to

4. combine well. Enjoy!

39.Braised Chicken with Olives

Total time: 1 hour 50 minutes

Prep time: 20 minutes

Cook time: 1 hour 30 minutes

Yield: 4 servings

Ingredients

1 tbsp. extra virgin olive oil

4 whole skinned chicken legs, cut into drumsticks and thighs

1 cup low-sodium canned chicken broth

1 cup dry white wine

4 sprigs thyme

2 tbsp. chopped fresh ginger

2 garlic cloves, minced

3 carrots, diced

1 medium yellow onion, diced

3/4¾ cup chickpeas, drained, rinsed

½ cup green olives, pitted and roughly chopped

⅓ cup raisins

1 cup water

Directions

1. Preheat your oven to 350°F.

2. Heat extra virgin olive oil in a Dutch oven or a large ovenproof skillet over

3. medium heat.

4. Add the chicken pieces into the skillet and sauté for about 5minutes per side

5. or until browned and crisped on both sides.

6. Transfer the cooked chicken to a plate and set aside.

7. Lower heat to medium low and add garlic, onion, carrots, and ginger to the

8. same skillet; cook, stirring, for about 5 minutes or until onion is translucent

9. and tender.

10. Stir in water, chicken broth, and wine; bring the mixture to a

gentle boil.

11. Return the chicken to the pot and stir in thyme.

12. Bring the mixture back the boil and cover.

13. Transfer to the oven and braise for about 45 minutes.

14. Remove the pot from the oven and stir in chickpeas, olives, and raisins.

15. Return to oven and braise, uncovered, for 20 minutes more.

16. Remove the skillet from oven and discard thyme.

17. Serve immediately.

40.Healthy Greek Dip

Total time: 25 minutes

Prep time: 25 minutes

Cook time: 0 minutes

Yield: 8 servings

Ingredients

½ cup feta cheese, crumbled

½ a liter lemon yogurt

1 tsp. freshly squeezed lemon juice

Sea salt, to taste

1 cup plain hummus

½ cup tomatoes, seeded and chopped

½ cup finely chopped English cucumber

½ cup Kalamata olives, pitted and chopped

2 tbsp. chopped green onions

1 tbsp. chopped fresh parsley

Directions

1. Mix cheese, yogurt, lemon juice and salt in a small bowl.

2. Line up 8 glasses and layer 2 tablespoons hummus, 1 teaspoon tomato, 1

3. tablespoon of yogurt mixture, 1 tablespoon of cucumber, I tablespoon

4. olives and 1 teaspoon green onions.

5. Top with the remaining ingredients.

41.Mediterranean Salsa

Total time: 20 minutes

Prep time: 20 minutes

Cook time: 0 minutes

Yield: 6 servings

Ingredients

1 cup zucchini, finely chopped

1 ½ cups tomatoes, seeded and chopped

½ cup roasted bell peppers, finely chopped

1 garlic clove, minced

1 ½ tsp. capers

1 tbsp. fresh flat leaf parsley, chopped

1 tbsp. fresh basil, chopped

2 tbsp. red onion, finely chopped

2 tsp. lemon juice

2 tsp. extra virgin olive oil

A pinch of sea salt

A pinch of black pepper, freshly ground

Directions

1. Combine all ingredients in a bowl and serve immediately or refrigerate.

42.Mediterranean Tapenade

Total time: 5 minutes

Prep time: 5 minutes

Cook time: 0 minutes

Yield: 8 servings

Ingredients

1 cup Kalamata olives, pitted

Juice of 1 lemon

2 tbsp. extra virgin olive oil

5 cloves garlic

¼ cup parsley, chopped

1 tbsp. capers

½ tsp. allspice

Directions

1. Place all the ingredients in a food processor and process till they combined

2. well.

3. Serve in 8 small bowls.

43.Mango Salsa

Total time: 20 minutes

Prep time: 20 minutes

Cook time: 0 minutes

Yield: 4 servings

Ingredients

1 cup cucumber, chopped

2 cups mango, diced

½ cup cilantro, minced

2 tbsp. fresh lime juice

1 tbsp. scallions, minced

¼ tsp. chipotle powder

¼ tsp. sea salt

Directions

1. Mix together all ingredients in a bowl and serve or refrigerate.

44. Tzatziki

Total time: 26 minutes

Prep time: 20 minutes

Cook time: 6 minutes

Refrigerator time: At least 6 hours

Yield: 32 servings

Ingredients

32 ounces plain Greek yogurt

5 cloves garlic, minced

1 English cucumber, peeled and grated

¼ cup olive oil

3 tbsp. distilled white vinegar

Sea salt

Directions

1. Cover a medium bowl with a cheesecloth and strain the yogurt in the fridge

2. for 6 hours or better still, overnight.

3. Also drain as much water from the garlic and cucumber.

4. Mix all the ingredients and stir until a thick mixture forms.

45.Mediterranean Kale

Total time: 25 minutes

Prep time: 15 minutes

Cook time: 10 minutes

Yields: 6 servings

Ingredients

12 cups chopped kale

1 tsp. soy sauce

1 tbsp. minced garlic

1 tbsp. olive oil or as needed

2 tbsp. lemon juice

A pinch salt

A pinch freshly ground black pepper

Directions

1. Add water to cover the bottom of a medium-sized saucepan; add steamer

2. insert.

3. Cover and bring the water to a boil.

4. Add kale, cover and steam for about 10 minutes or until just tender.

5. In a large bowl, whisk together soy sauce, garlic, olive oil, lemon juice, salt

6. and pepper.

7. Add the steamed kale to the bowl and toss until well coated.

46.Leeky Parsley Soup

Total time: 35 minutes

Prep time: 20 minutes

Cook time: 15 minutes

Yields: 4 to 6 servings

Ingredients

1 tbsp. olive oil

1 bunch fresh flat-leaf parsley, stems chopped, parsley leaves reserved for

garnishing

2 large or 3 medium leeks, pale green and white parts chopped

4 cups of water

4 cups low-sodium vegetable or chicken broth or 4 cups of water

4 green onions (about 3-inch green parts and white parts), chopped

1 medium unpeeled zucchini, shredded with a grater

2 tsp. salt

Directions

1. Add oil to a large stockpot set over medium high heat.

2. Add parsley and the leeks to the oil and cook, stirring continuously for

3. about 5 minutes or until leeks become light in color.

4. Add broth or water, green onions and zucchini and bring the mixture to a

5. boil.

6. Lower heat to medium and simmer for about 10 minutes.

7. Remove from heat and cool the soup for about 10 minutes.

8. Serve warm, garnished with parsley leaves.

47.Tasty Lentil Soup

Total time: 1 hour 20 minutes

Prep time: 20 minutes

Cook time: 1 hour

Yield: 4 servings

Ingredients

1 ½ cups brown lentils

¼ cup olive oil

1 large onion, chopped

2 cloves garlic, pressed

1 carrot, chopped

¼ tsp. dried oregano

¼ tsp. dried rosemary

2 bay leaves, dried

1 tbsp. tomato paste

1 tsp. red wine vinegar

Directions

1. Pour the lentils in a large saucepan and cover with water.

2. Place over medium heat and bring to a boil; cook for 10 – 20 minutes and

3. drain in a strainer.

4. Clean the saucepan and pour in the olive oil and bring to medium heat.

5. Add the onions and garlic and cook until the onions are soft, then add the

6. carrots and cook for a further 5 minutes.

7. Pour in the lentils and 1 ½ cups of water, oregano, rosemary and bay leaves.

8. Once the pan comes to a boil, reduce the heat and simmer for 10 minutes.

9. Add the tomato paste and continue simmering until the lentils soften for

10. about 30 minutes stirring.

11. Add water to get the consistency of soup you like.

12. Drizzle with the vinegar to taste.

48. Veggie Barley Soup

Total time: 1 hour 45 minutes

Prep time: 15 minutes

Cook time: 1 hour 30 minutes

Yield: 4 servings

Ingredients

2 quarts vegetable broth

2 stalks celery, chopped

2 large carrots, chopped

1 cup barley

1 (15 ounce) can garbanzo beans, drained

1 zucchini, chopped

1 (14.5 ounce) can tomatoes with juice

1 onion, chopped

3 bay leaves

1 tsp. dried parsley

1 tsp. white sugar

1 tsp. garlic powder

1 tsp. Worcestershire sauce

1 tsp. paprika

1 tsp. curry powder

½ tsp. ground black pepper

1 tsp. sea salt

Directions

1. Add broth to a large soup pot over medium heat.

2. Stir in celery, carrots, barley, garbanzo beans, zucchini, tomatoes, onion,

3. bay leaves, parsley, sugar, garlic powder, Worcestershire sauce, paprika,

4. curry powder, sea salt and pepper.

5. Bring the mixture to a gentle boil; cover and lower heat to

medium low.

6. Cook for about 90 minutes or until the soup is thick.

7. Discard bay leaves and serve hot.

49.Chickpea Soup

Total time: 50 minutes

Prep time: 20 minutes

Cook time: 30 minutes

Yield: 6 servings

Ingredients

1 tbsp. extra virgin olive oil

4 cloves garlic, minced

1 cup diced onion

2 (15-oz.) cans chickpeas, rinsed, drained

¼ cup freshly squeezed lemon juice

½ cup chopped parsley

1 bay leaf

1 ½ tsp. sea salt

Moroccan Spice Oil

Directions

1. Heat extra virgin olive oil in a medium saucepan set over medium heat; add

2. garlic and onion and sauté, stirring, for about 10 minutes or until starts to

3. brown.

4. Add 4 cups of water, chickpeas, parsley and bay leaf; stir and bring to a

5. gentle boil, covered.

6. Reduce heat and simmer for about 15 minutes.

7. Stir in sea salt and discard bay leaf.

8. In batches, puree the soup in a food processor until very smooth and

9. creamy.

10. Return the pureed soup back to the pan and stir in lemon juice.

11. Ladle the soup into bowls and drizzle with about ½ teaspoon Moroccan

12. Spice Oil and sprinkle with parsley.

13. Enjoy!

50.Red Lentil Bean Soup

Total time: 1 hour

Prep time: 15 minutes

Cook time: 45 minutes

Yield: 4 servings

Ingredients

2 cups dried red lentil beans, rinsed

2 tbsp. extra virgin olive oil, plus more for drizzling

2 large onions, diced

1 - 2 finely chopped carrots

8 cups chicken stock

2 ripe tomatoes, cubed

1 tsp. ground cumin

Sea salt

Black pepper

2 cups fresh spinach

Directions

1. Soak lentils for at least 2 hours.

2. In a pot set over medium high heat, boil the lentils until almost cooked.

3. In a soup pot, heat extra virgin olive oil over medium heat; add diced

4. onions and carrots and sauté for about 4 minutes or until tender.

5. Add stock, tomatoes, cumin, sea salt and pepper and simmer for about 40

6. minutes or until lentils are tender.

7. Stir in spinach until just wilted and drizzle with extra virgin olive oil just

8. before serving.

CPSIA information can be obtained
at www.ICGtesting.com
Printed in the USA
BVHW091033100621
609274BV00001B/124